THE CELLO ETUDE SYSTEM

Part 0:
Beginning Studies
SOLO BOOK

compiled and written
by Cassia Harvey

The Cello Etude System, Part 0: Beginning Studies, DUET SCORE
(the accompaniment part for this book) is also available: CHP411

CHP410

©2021 C. Harvey Publications
All Rights Reserved.
www.charveypublications.com - print books
www.learnstrings.com - downloadable books
www.harveystringarrangements.com - chamber music

Table of Contents

Section   **Page**

What's In the Book... iv
The Purpose of Etudes..................................... iv
How This Series Got Started............................. iv
How to Practice Using This Book...................... v
Accelerated Etude Path.................................... v
Book 0: Goals for Study................................... v
Complete List of Etudes................................ vi
Etudes, Part One: Open String Studies................ 2
Etudes, Part Two: Studies with First Finger.......... 16
Etudes, Part Three: Learning the Notes on Each String.... 19
Etudes, Part Four: Studies Across All Four Strings....... 43
Index of Composers....................................... 73
Index of Main Skills in Each Etude................... 74

What's In the Book

Rare and Classic Cello Etudes

Many of these etudes are extremely rare while others are well-known classic cello studies by the great teachers of the past. The etudes have been put in approximate order of difficulty and grouped so that they teach and review essential cello skills.

Two Paths Through the Book

- *Relaxed Learners* can play through the book as written.
- *Accelerated Learners* can use the guides at the bottom of the etudes to chart a faster course.

The Purpose of Etudes

Etudes are a bridge between exercises and repertoire, incorporating both technique and musicality to teach one or more specific skills. Because technical exercises often fall short in teaching rhythm, dynamics, etc., **etudes are an essential part of every practice session.** The duet parts to these etudes let the teacher lead rhythmically and expressively and help their student learn the skills they will need to play in chamber groups or orchestras.

How This Series Got Started

When I started teaching, I used all of the well-known cello etude books with my students, including Dotzauer, Schroeder, and Lee. But over the years, I was surprised to find just how many more amazing etudes had been written! These etudes were unknown, out of print, and almost impossible to find. I started collecting etudes, making copies, and distributing them to my students. As my studio room started filling up with all of these books, I realized that I was assigning just a few etudes from each book before moving to another book. This just wasn't practical and certainly wasn't replicable to other teaching studios. So I started compiling the etudes, grouping them by skill, and putting them in order of difficulty (as much as possible.) I wanted this series to be both a **resource** and a **practical system** through the etudes that my students and I have been studying for many years. The relaxed and accelerated learning paths can accommodate students with different learning styles and the teacher is encouraged to further chart their own path through each book with their students.

©2021 C. Harvey Publications All Rights Reserved.

How to Practice Using This Book

- Etudes should be practiced after exercises and scales and before repertoire.
- This book consists of short etudes at or close to the same level, only incrementally increasing in difficulty. *Because of this, teachers should assign multiple etudes each week, whenever possible.* This book was designed to be studied at a somewhat quicker pace than most other etude books.
- By playing through multiple etudes each week, **students will build essential sight-reading skills** from the very beginning.
- Relaxed learners can play through the entire book. Accelerated learners should use the cues below the etudes to chart their path through the book. See below for more about the accelerated path.
- The **Duet accompaniment score** for this book is available separately: **CHP411**.

Accelerated Etude Path

- Students who learn more quickly, who are on an advanced learning trajectory, or who have easily mastered the material should use the accelerated learning path.
- The accelerated learning path teaches the same concepts as the relaxed learning path but has less review and repetition.
- If you are unsure whether the relaxed or accelerated path is right for you, start on the relaxed path and switch to the accelerated path if the etudes start to feel too easy.

Book 0: Goals for Study

Learn the notes in closed first position.

Learn and apply slurs and ties to different note groupings.

Learn rhythms in 4/4, 3/4, and 6/8 time signatures.

Learn and use different bow lengths and different bow speeds to play with correct rhythm.

Learn and use staccato bowing.

Learn and use pickup notes.

©2021 C. Harvey Publications All Rights Reserved.

☐ = Accelerated Path

Complete List of Etudes - Page 1

Etude	Title	Composer	THIS BOOK Solo Page	Duet Page
1	Focus on the Upper Strings	Wichtl, G.	2	2
2	Focus on the Lower Strings	Harvey C.	2	3
3	Four Miniatures for Building Tone	Werner, J.	3	4
4	Four Miniatures with Double Stops	Fuchs, C.	3	5
5	Bow Speed and String Crossing	Schröder, C.	4	6
6	Slow Up-Bows	Wichtl, G.	4	8
7	Bow Rhythms	Davidov, K.	5	9
8	Subdividing Rhythms	Verrimst, V.	6	10
9	String Crossing in 3/4	Kummer, F.	7	11
10	Slow Syncopation	Wichtl, G.	7	12
11	Uneven Bow Speeds	Wichtl, G.	8	13
12	String-Crossing Exercise for No. 13	Harvey, C.	8	14
13	Extreme String Crossing	Liégeois, C.	8	14
14	First Dynamics	Harvey, M.	9	16
15	Slur Practice	Harvey, C.	9	16
16	Slow Slur Etude	Bornschein, F.	10	17
17	Quarter Note Slur Practice	Harvey, C.	11	18
18	Slur Etude	Schiffer, A.	11	18
19	Double Stop Etude	Harvey, C.	12	19
20	Bow Rhythms and String Crossing	Harvey, C.	12	20
21	Rhythm Etude with Slurs	Harvey, C.	13	21
22	Dotted Quarter Notes in 6/8	Harvey, C.	13	22
23	6/8 Timing	Harvey, C.	14	23
24	Triplets and Sixteenth Notes	Harvey, C.	14	24
25	Open-String Rhythm Study	Verrimst, V.	15	25
26	First Finger Notes	Harvey, C.	16	26
27	First Finger on A and D	Harvey, C.	16	27
28	First Finger on All Four Strings	Harvey, C.	17	28
29	Slurs and First Finger	Harvey, C.	18	29
30	First Finger Study for Tone	Harvey, C.	18	30

☐ = Accelerated Path

Complete List of Etudes - Page 2

Etude	Title	Composer	THIS BOOK Solo Page	Duet Page
31	A-String Etude No. 1	Nölck, A.	19	31
32	A-String Etude No. 2	Romberg, B.	19	32
33	A-String Etude No. 3	Davidov, K.	20	32
34	A-String Skipping Study	Romberg, B.	20	33
35	A-String Rhythmic Etude	Harvey, C.	20	33
36	Slurs and Rhythm	Schiffer, A.	21	34
37	Study for Learning C-natural and C-sharp	Harvey, C.	21	35
38	C-natural and C-sharp Study	Harvey, C.	22	36
39	Bow Speed Study	Davidov, K.	22	37
40	D-String Study	Bornschein, F.	23	38
41	Little March Etude	Harvey, C.	24	39
42	Slur Etude with Second Finger	Bornschein, F.	24	40
43	Agility Study	Harvey, C.	25	41
44	Up-Bow Etude with String Crossing	Bornschein, F.	25	42
45	Tone Etude	Nölck, A.	26	43
46	Melodic Etude in D Minor	Schiffer, A.	26	44
47	Melodic Etude in D major	Schiffer, A.	27	45
48	Slurs and F-sharp	Harvey, C.	27	46
49	Etude for Slur Coordination	Bornschein, F.	28	47
50	Three in a Bow	Harvey, C.	28	48
51	Etude Valsette	Bornschein, F.	28	48
52	Finger Twister	Davidov, K.	29	50
53	G-String Study	Nölck, A.	30	50
54	G-String Bow Speed Study	Harvey, C.	30	51
55	G-String Agility Study	Harvey, C.	30	51
56	Etude in 6/8 Timing	Harvey, C.	31	52
57	Learning B-flat on the G-String	Harvey, C.	31	52
58	B-flat Etude	Davidov, K.	31	53
59	C-String Study for Tone	Nölck, A.	32	53
60	6/8 Study on the C-String	Harvey, C.	32	54

☐ = Accelerated Path

Complete List of Etudes - Page 3

Etude	Title	Composer	THIS BOOK Solo Page	Duet Page
61	Bow Speed Study	Wichtl, G.	32	54
62	Melodic C-String Etude	Harvey, C.	33	55
63	D-sharp and E-flat	Harvey, C.	33	56
64	Note-Reading Study	Davidov, K.	34	56
65	G and C-String Study	Harvey, C.	34	57
66	Double Stop Practice	Harvey, C.	34	57
67	Double Stops in 3/4	Bornschein, F.	35	58
68	Across Strings	Harvey, C.	36	59
69	Slur Study	Bornschein, F.	36	59
70	Learning Pickup Notes	Harvey, C.	37	60
71	The Pickup Note Study	Harvey, C.	37	61
72	Etude for Rhythm and Tone	Fuchs, C.	38	62
73	3/4 Timing with Slurs	Bornschein, F.	38	63
74	Waltz Study No. 1	Whitehouse, W.E.	39	64
75	Waltz Study No. 2	Whitehouse, W.E.	39	65
76	Intonation Etude	Fuchs, C.	40	66
77	Double Stop Etude	Romberg, B.	40	67
78	Staccato and First and Second Endings	Nölck, A.	41	68
79	Arpeggio Etude	Romberg, B.	42	70
80	Bowing Study	Harvey, C.	42	71
81	Bowing Workout Etude	Mazas, J.	42	72
82	Second Finger Agility Etude	Harvey, C.	43	73
83	Note-Reading and Dynamics	Cousin, E.	44	74
84	6/8 in C Major	Harvey, C.	45	76
85	Study on Retaking	Harvey, C.	45	77
86	Second and Third Finger Review	Harvey, C.	46	78
87	C Major Study	Schröder, C.	46	78
88	Intonation Exercise	Harvey, C.	47	80
89	Double Stop Etude	Harvey, C.	47	80
90	Using Fourth Finger in C Major	Harvey, C.	48	81

☐ = Accelerated Path

Complete List of Etudes - Page 4

Etude	Title	Composer	THIS BOOK Solo Page	Duet Page
91	Bow Speed Study	Kummer, F.	48	82
92	Bow Speed in 3/4 Timing	de Swert, J.	49	83
93	Counting Half Notes	van Rooijen, N.	50	84
94	Tone Etude	Nölck, A.	51	85
95	Up-Bow Etude	Mollier, P.	51	86
96	Retaking for Up-Bow Pickups	Mollier, P.	52	87
97	Study on Pickup Notes	van Rooijen, N.	52	88
98	Study for Speed	Cuccoli, A.	53	90
99	Melodic Etude	Chevillard, A.	55	92
100	Study on Ties	Gruet, A.	56	94
101	Slurs and Dynamics	Liégeois, C.	57	96
102	6/8 Speed and Agility	Duport, J.	58	98
103	Focus on Bow Speed	Cuccoli, A.	58	100
104	Arpeggio Etude with Staccato	Cuccoli, A.	60	102
105	Double Stop Etude	Paschalski, K.	60	103
106	String Crossing	Cousin, E.	61	104
107	Slurs Across Bar Lines	Cousin, E.	62	106
108	Introduction to G Major	Harvey, C.	63	108
109	Slur Patterns in G Major	Fuchs, C.	63	108
110	Bow Direction Study	Uberti, V.	64	109
111	Bow Retaking Study	Mollier, P.	64	110
112	Study in 7/4	Harvey, C.	65	111
113	G Major Staccato Study	Depas, E.	66	112
114	G Major Double Stop Etude	de Swert, J.	66	113
115	Second and Third Finger	Harvey, C.	68	114
116	Learning a Slow Up-Bow	Harvey, C.	68	114
117	Etude in Folk Style	Bornschein, F.	68	114
118	Slurs and Rhythm	Goodban, H	70	116
119	Bow Rhythm Etude	Cuccoli, A.	71	118
120	Rhythmic Etude	Stiastny, B.	72	120

Part One: Open String Studies

1. Focus on the Upper Strings

G. Wichtl, arr. Harvey

2. Focus on the Lower Strings

C. Harvey

©2021 C. Harvey Publications All Rights Reserved

3. Four Miniatures for Building Tone

J. Werner

4. Four Miniatures with Double Stops

C. Fuchs, arr. Harvey

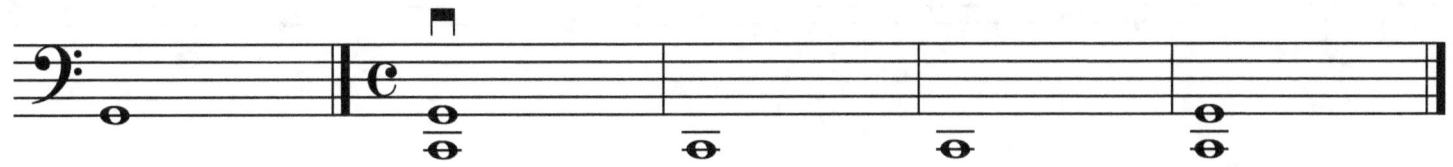

5. Bow Speed and String Crossing

C. Schröder

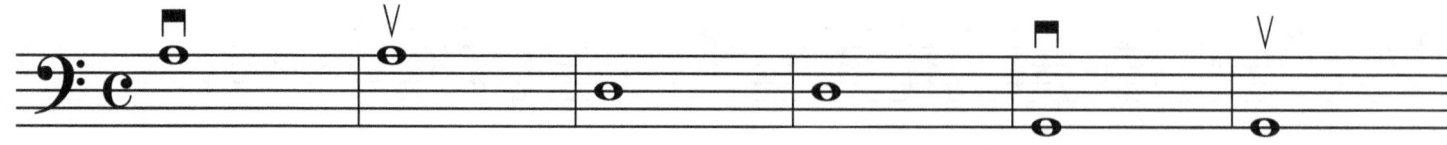

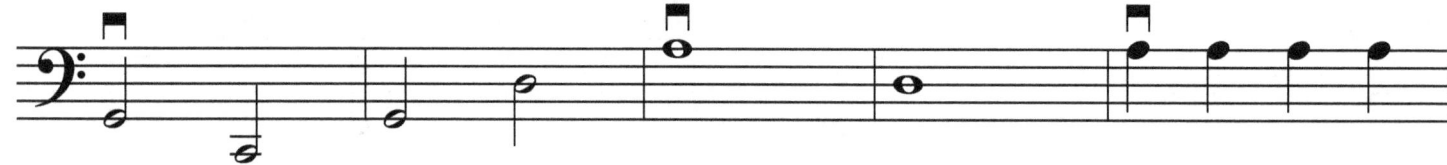

6. Slow Up-Bows

G. Wichtl, arr. Harvey

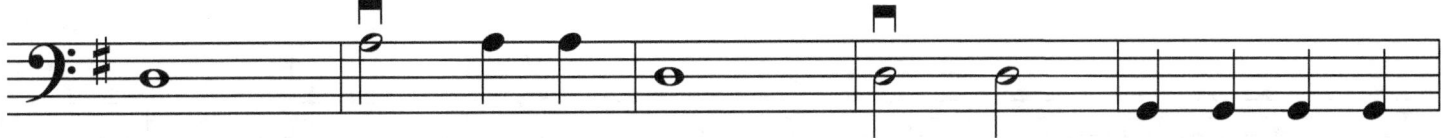

7. Bow Rhythms

K. Davidov, arr. Harvey

8. Subdividing Rhythms

V. Verrimst, arr. Harvey

Cello Etude System, Book 0: Solo Book

9. String Crossing in 3/4

F. Kummer

Accelerated students may skip to No. 16.

10. Slow Syncopation

G. Wichtl, arr. Harvey

©2021 C. Harvey Publications All Rights Reserved

11. Uneven Bow Speeds

G. Wichtl, arr. Harvey

12. String Crossing Exercise for No. 13

C. Harvey

13. Extreme String Crossing!

C. Liégeois

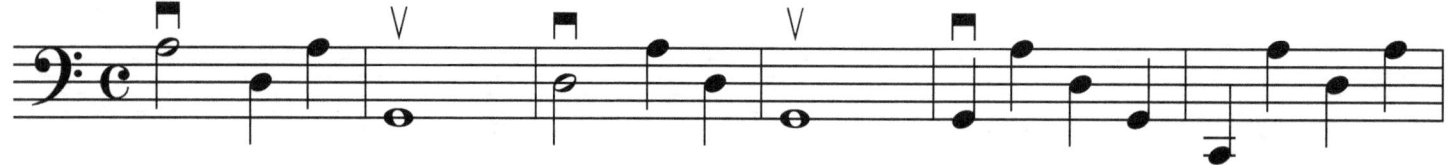
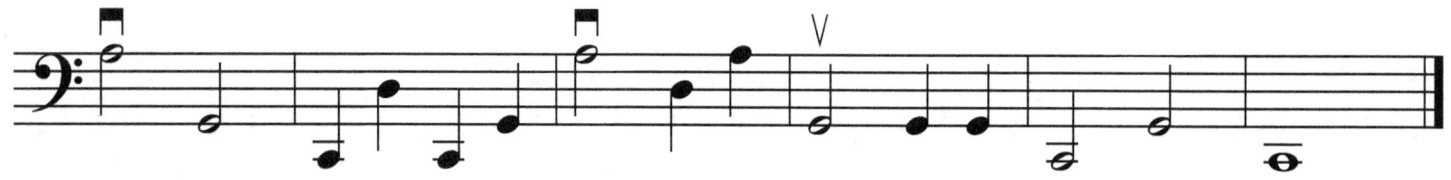

14. First Dynamics

M. Harvey

15. Slur Practice

C. Harvey

©2021 C. Harvey Publications All Rights Reserved

16. Slow Slur Etude

F. Bornschein

Cello Etude System, Book 0: Solo Book
11

17. Quarter Note Slur Practice

C. Harvey

18. Slur Etude

A. Schiffer

Accelerated students may skip to No. 21.

©2021 C. Harvey Publications All Rights Reserved

19. Double Stop Etude

C. Harvey

20. Bow Rhythms and String Crossing

C. Harvey

Cello Etude System, Book 0: Solo Book

21. Rhythm Etude with Slurs

C. Harvey

22. Dotted Quarter Notes in 6/8

C. Harvey

Accelerated students may skip to No. 25.

©2021 C. Harvey Publications All Rights Reserved

23. 6/8 Timing

C. Harvey

24. Triplets and Sixteenth Notes

C. Harvey

25. Open-String Rhythm Study

V. Verrimst

Part Two: Studies with First Finger

26. First Finger Notes

C. Harvey

27. First Finger on A and D

C. Harvey

28. First Finger on All Four Strings

C. Harvey

29. Slurs and First Finger

C. Harvey

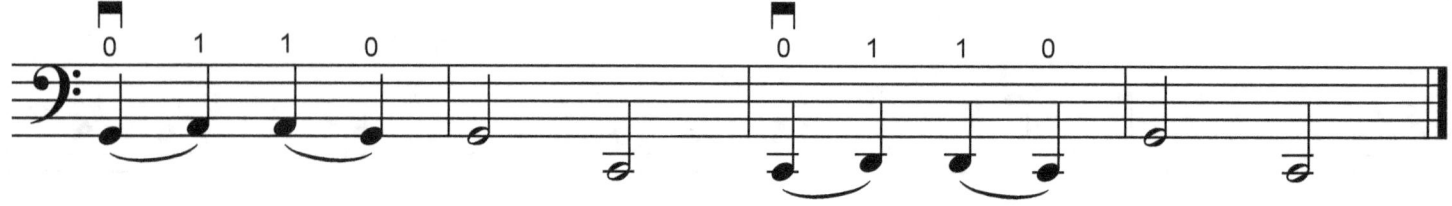

Accelerated students may skip to No. 31.

30. First Finger Study for Tone

C. Harvey

©2021 C. Harvey Publications All Rights Reserved

Cello Etude System, Book 0: Solo Book

Part Three: Learning the Notes on Each String

31. A-String Etude No. 1

A. Nölck

Accelerated students may skip to No. 36.

32. A-String Etude No. 2

B. Romberg

©2021 C. Harvey Publications All Rights Reserved

33. A-String Etude No. 3

K. Davidov

34. A-String Skipping Study

B. Romberg

35. A-String Rhythmic Etude

C. Harvey

©2021 C. Harvey Publications All Rights Reserved

36. Slurs and Rhythm

A. Schiffer

Accelerated students may skip to No. 38.

37. Study for Learning C♮ and C♯

C. Harvey

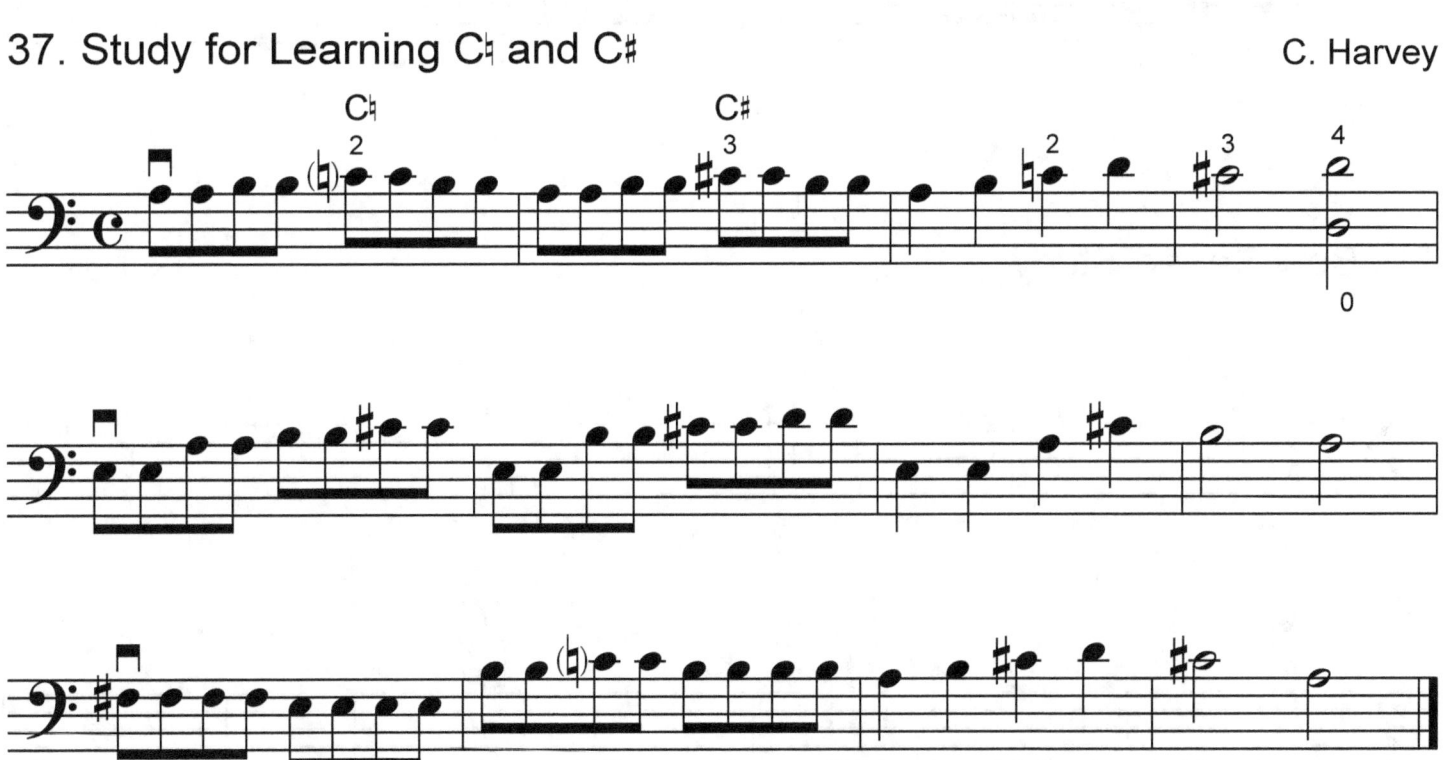

38. C♮ and C♯ Study

F. Bornschein

39. Bow Speed Study

K. Davidov

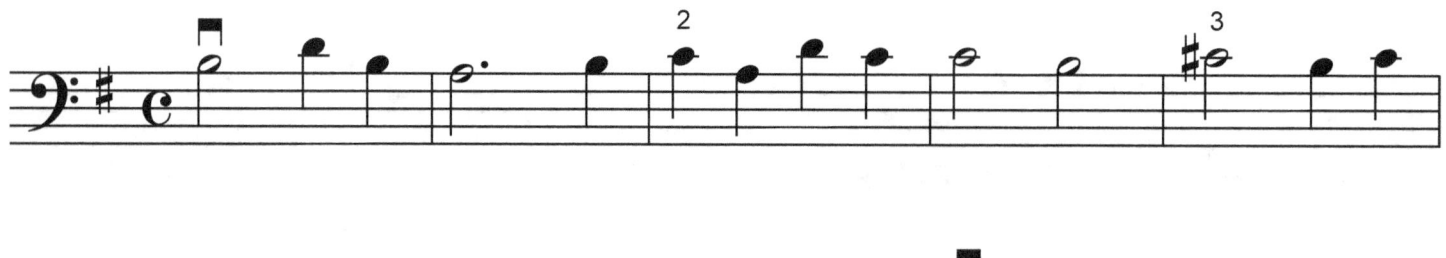

40. D-String Study
F. Bornschein

Accelerated students may skip to No. 42.

41. Little March Etude

C. Harvey

42. Slur Etude with Second Finger

F. Bornschein, arr. Harvey

Accelerated students may skip to No. 46.

©2021 C. Harvey Publications All Rights Reserved

43. Agility Study
C. Harvey

44. Up-Bow Etude with String Crossing
F. Bornschein

45. Tone Etude

A. Nölck

Use a whole bow for each note.

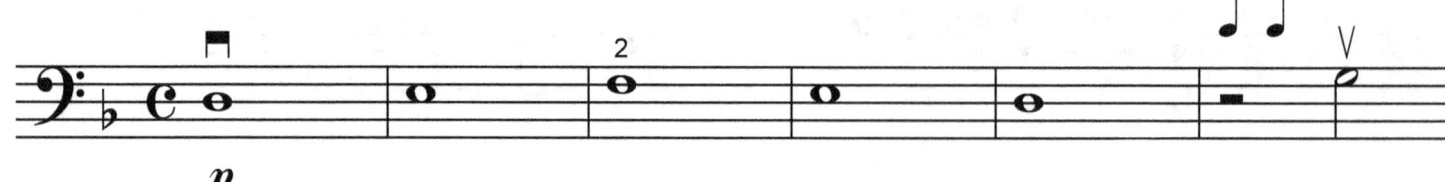
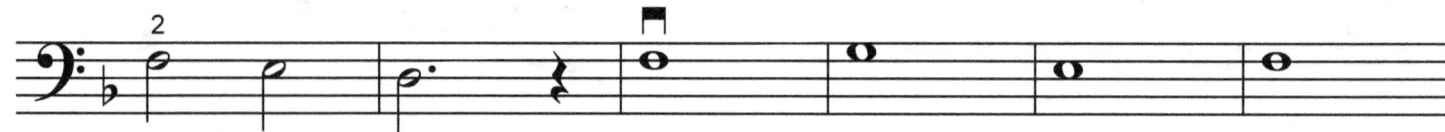

46. Melodic Etude in D Minor

A. Schiffer

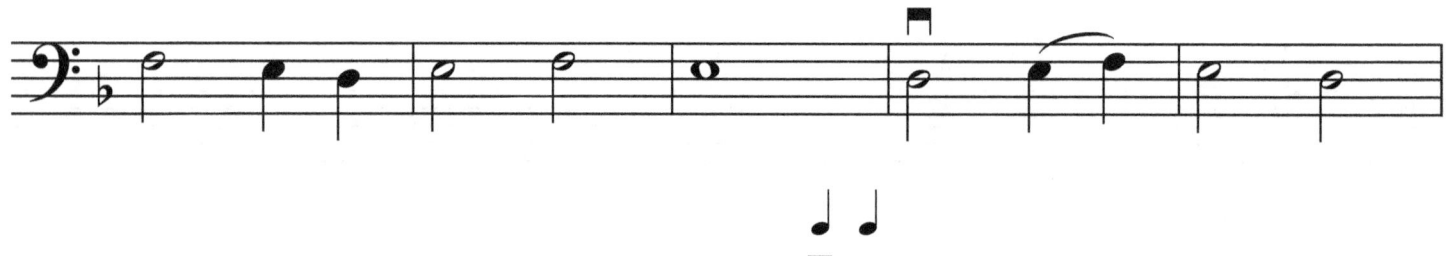

47. Melodic Etude in D Major

F♯ in the key signature tells you to play 3rd finger on the D string (F♯) for the entire etude.

A. Schiffer

Accelerated students may skip to No. 50.

48. Slurs and F♯

C. Harvey

49. Etude for Slur Coordination

F. Bornschein

50. Three in a Bow

C. Harvey

51. Etude Valsette

F. Bornschein

Cello Etude System, Book 0: Solo Book
29

52. Finger Twister
K. Davidov

These are played in the same place, by the same finger.

©2021 C. Harvey Publications All Rights Reserved

53. G-String Study

A. Nölck

Use a whole bow for each note.

Accelerated students may skip to No. 57.

54. G-String Bow Speed Study

C. Harvey

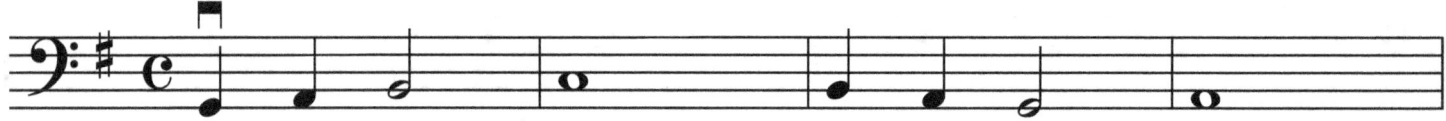

55. G-String Agility Study

C. Harvey

56. Etude in 6/8 Timing

C. Harvey

57. Learning B♭ on the G String

C. Harvey

58. B♭ Etude

K. Davidov

59. C-String Study for Tone

Use a whole bow for each note.

A. Nölck

60. 6/8 Study on the C-String

C. Harvey

61. Bow Speed Study

G. Wichtl, arr. Harvey

Accelerated students may skip to No. 65.

64. Note-Reading Study
K. Davidov

65. G and C-String Study
C. Harvey

Accelerated students may skip to No. 67.

66. Double Stop Practice
C. Harvey

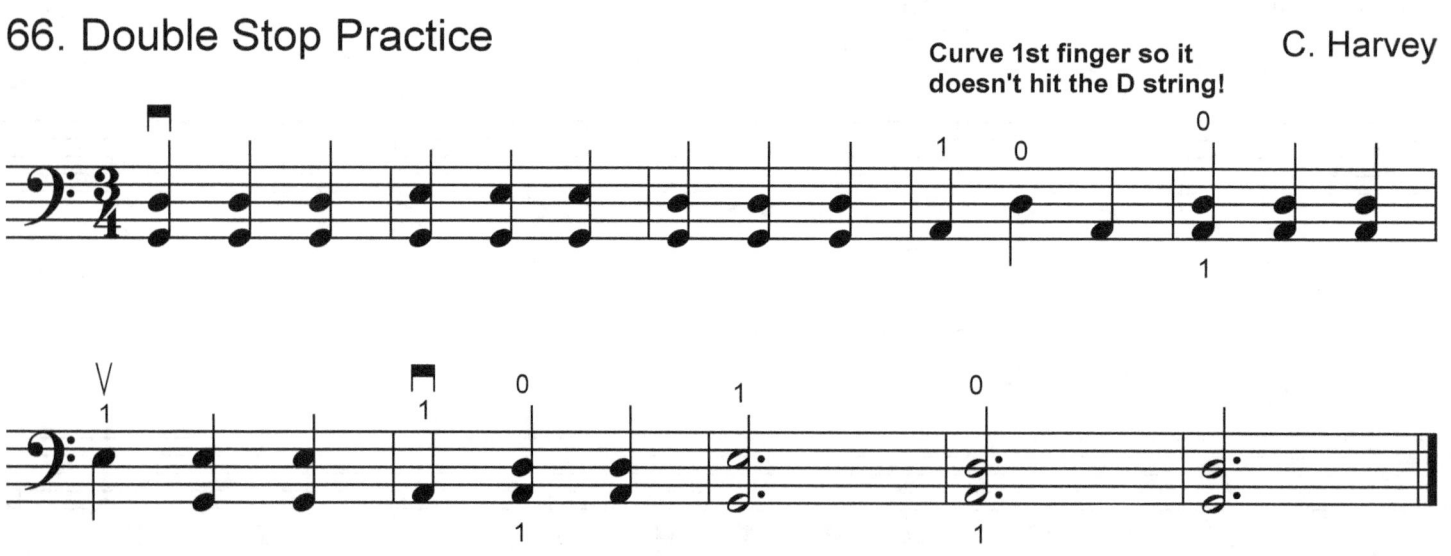

67. Double Stops in 3/4

F. Bornschein

Accelerated students may skip to No. 70.

68. Across Strings

C. Harvey

69. Slur Study

F. Bornschein

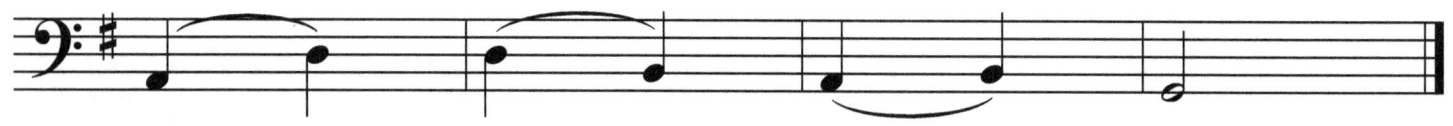

70. Learning Pickup Notes

C. Harvey

71. The Pickup Note Study

C. Harvey

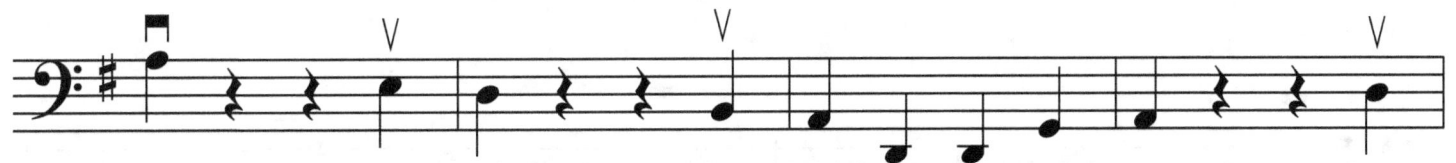

72. Etude for Rhythm and Tone

C. Fuchs

Accelerated students may skip to No. 78.

73. 3/4 Timing with Slurs

F. Bornschein

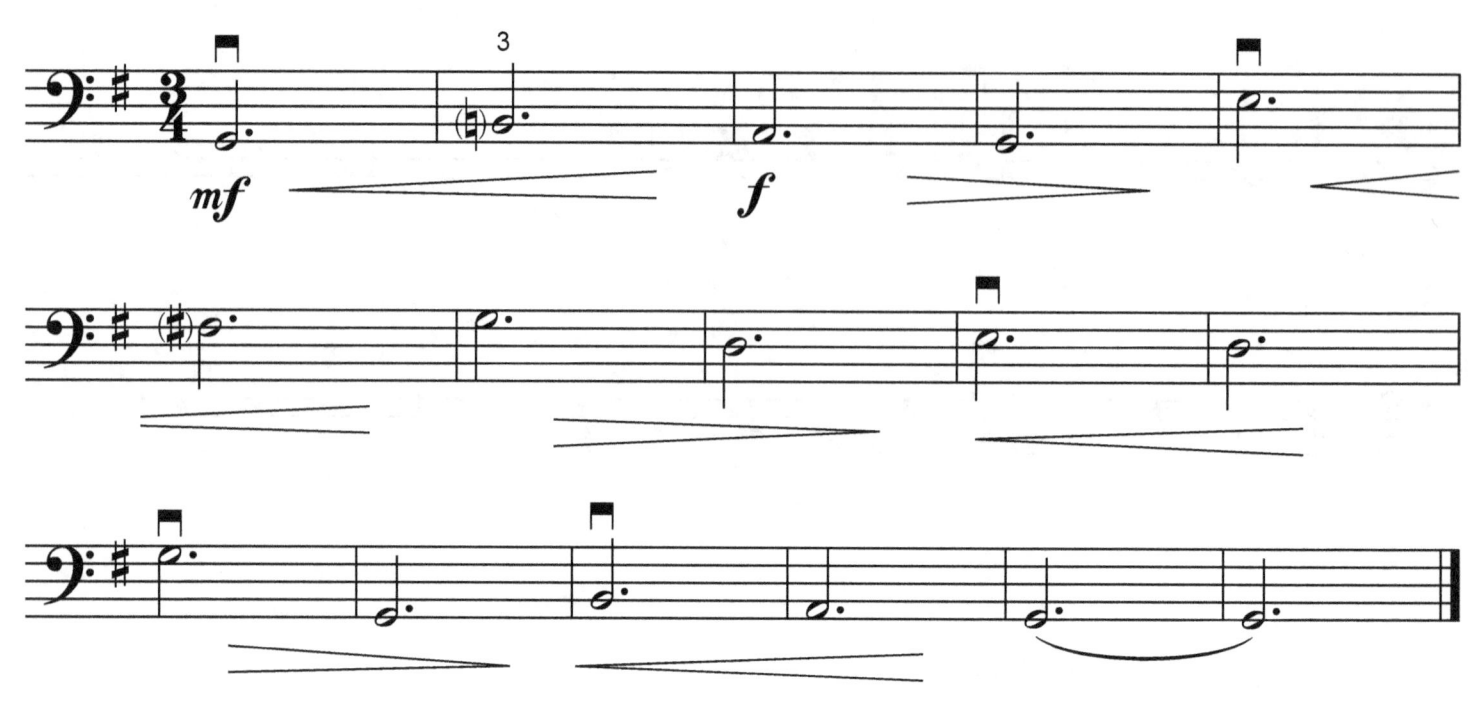

Cello Etude System, Book 0: Solo Book

74. Waltz Study No. 2

W. E. Whitehouse

75. Waltz Study No. 3

W. E. Whitehouse

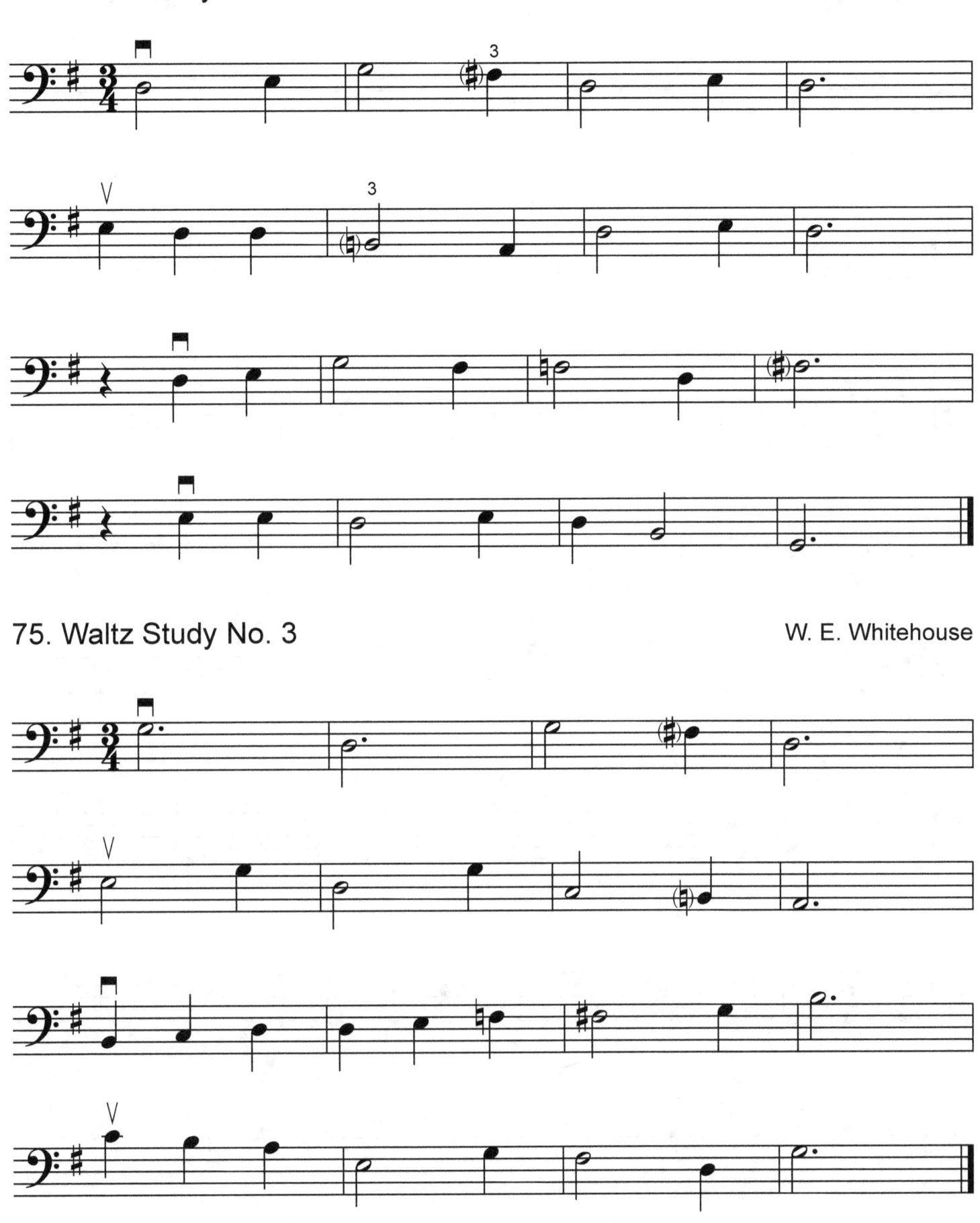

©2021 C. Harvey Publications All Rights Reserved

76. Intonation Etude

C. Fuchs, arr. Harvey

77. Double Stop Etude

B. Romberg, arr. Harvey

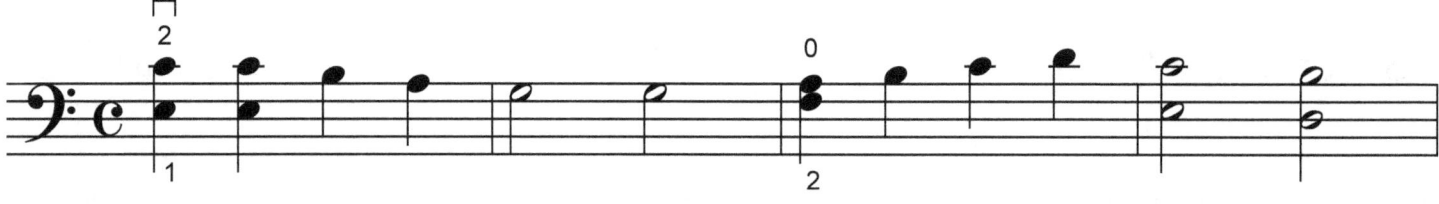

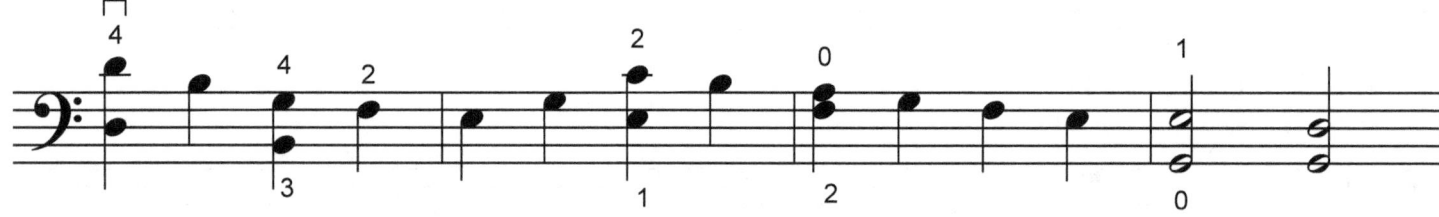

78. Staccato and First and Second Endings

A. Nölck

Part Four: Studies Across All Four Strings

82. Second Finger Agility Etude

C. Harvey

Accelerated students may skip to No. 87.

83. Note-Reading and Dynamics

E. Cousin

Cello Etude System, Book 0: Solo Book

84. 6/8 in C Major
C. Harvey

85. Study on Retaking
C. Harvey

©2021 C. Harvey Publications All Rights Reserved

86. Second and Third Finger Review

C. Harvey

87. C Major Study

C. Schröder

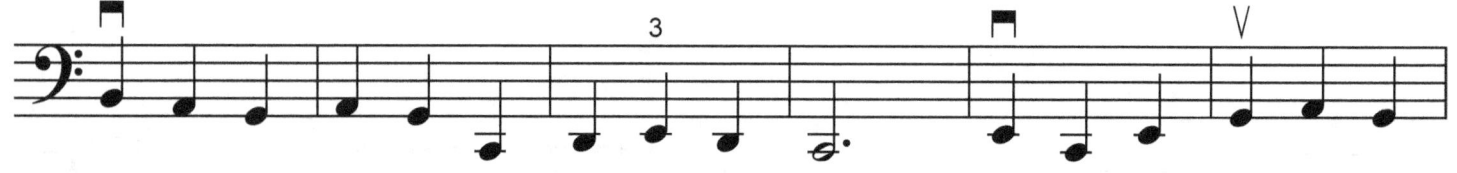

Cello Etude System, Book 0: Solo Book

88. Intonation Exercise

C. Harvey

89. Double Stop Etude

C. Harvey

©2021 C. Harvey Publications All Rights Reserved

90. Using Fourth Finger in C Major

C. Harvey

91. Bow Speed Study

F. Kummer

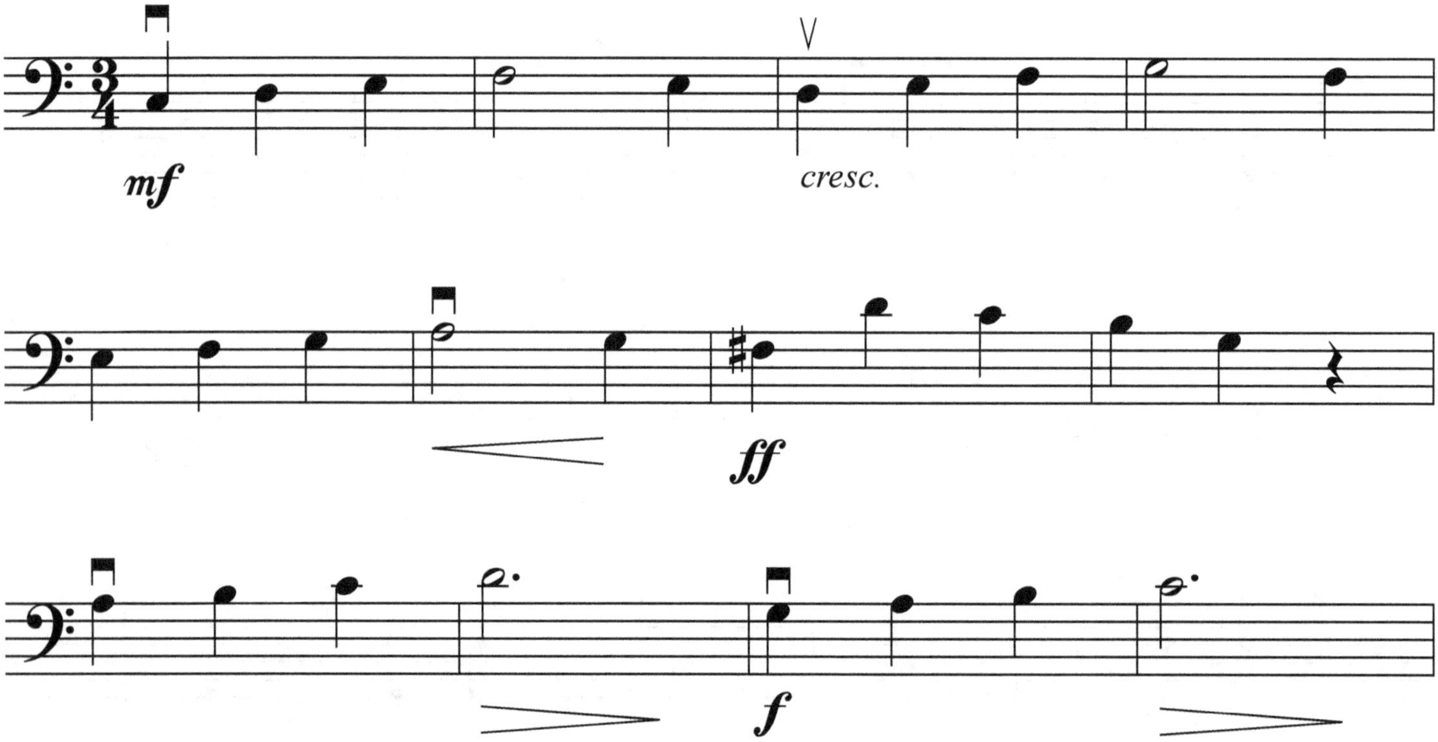

Cello Etude System, Book 0: Solo Book
49

92. Bow Speed in 3/4 Timing
J. de Swert

Accelerated students may skip to No. 95.

©2021 C. Harvey Publications All Rights Reserved

93. Counting Half Notes

N. van Rooijen

94. Tone Etude

A. Nölck

Use a whole bow for each note.

95. Up-Bow Etude

P. Mollier

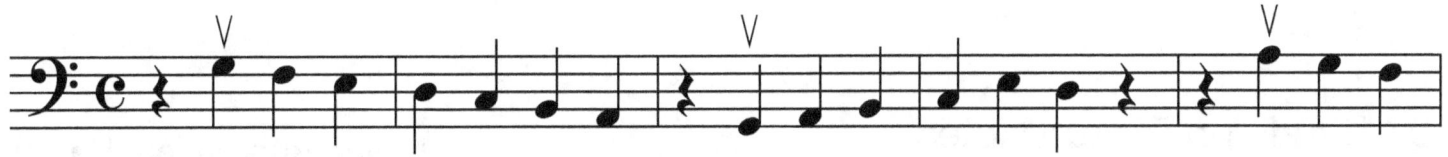

96. Retaking for Bow Pickups

P. Mollier, arr. Harvey

97. Study on Pickup Notes

N. van Rooijen, arr. Harvey

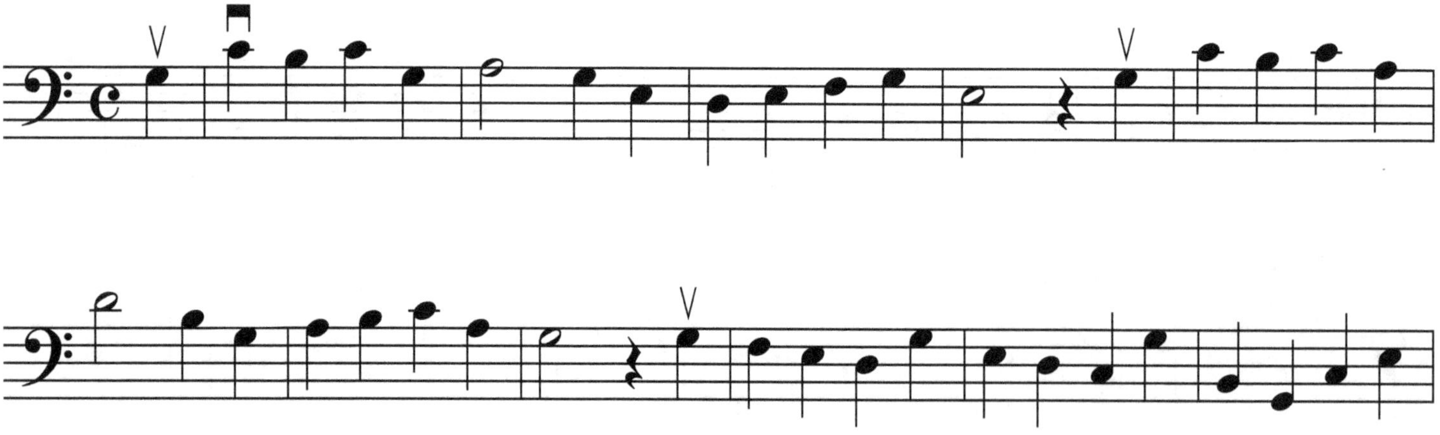

Cello Etude System, Book 0: Solo Book

Accelerated students may skip to No. 100.

98. Study for Speed

A. Cuccoli, arr. Harvey

Cello Etude System, Book 0: Solo Book

99. Melodic Etude

A. Chevillard, arr. Harvey

©2021 C. Harvey Publications All Rights Reserved

100. Study on Ties

A. Gruet

Cello Etude System, Book 0: Solo Book

101. Slurs and Dynamics

C. Liégeois

102. 6/8 Speed and Agility

J. Duport

Accelerated students may skip to No. 104.

103. Focus on Bow Speed

A. Cuccoli, arr. Harvey

Cello Etude System, Book 0: Solo Book

104. Arpeggio Etude with Staccato

A. Cuccoli, arr. Harvey

105. Double Stop Etude

K. Paschalski, arr. Harvey

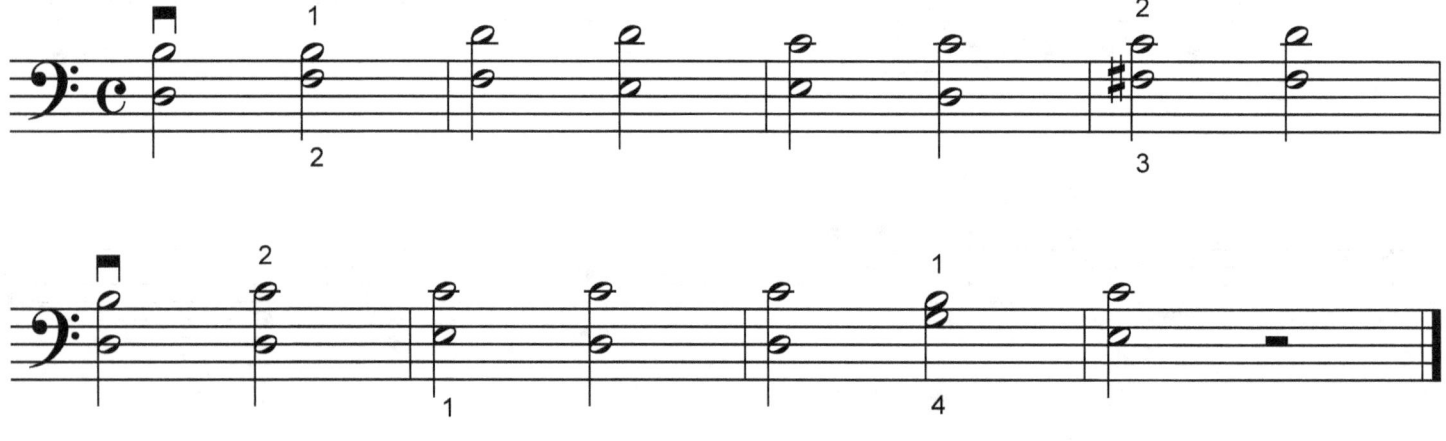

Cello Etude System, Book 0: Solo Book

106. String Crossing

E. Cousin, arr. Harvey

Accelerated students may skip to No. 108.

©2021 C. Harvey Publications All Rights Reserved

107. Slurs Across Bar Lines

E. Cousin, arr. Harvey

©2021 C. Harvey Publications All Rights Reserved

108. Introduction to G Major

C. Harvey

Accelerated students may skip to No. 110.

109. Slur Patterns in G Major

C. Fuchs, arr. Harvey

110. Bow Direction Study

V. Uberti, arr. Harvey

Accelerated students may skip to No. 112.

111. Bow Retaking Study

P. Mollier

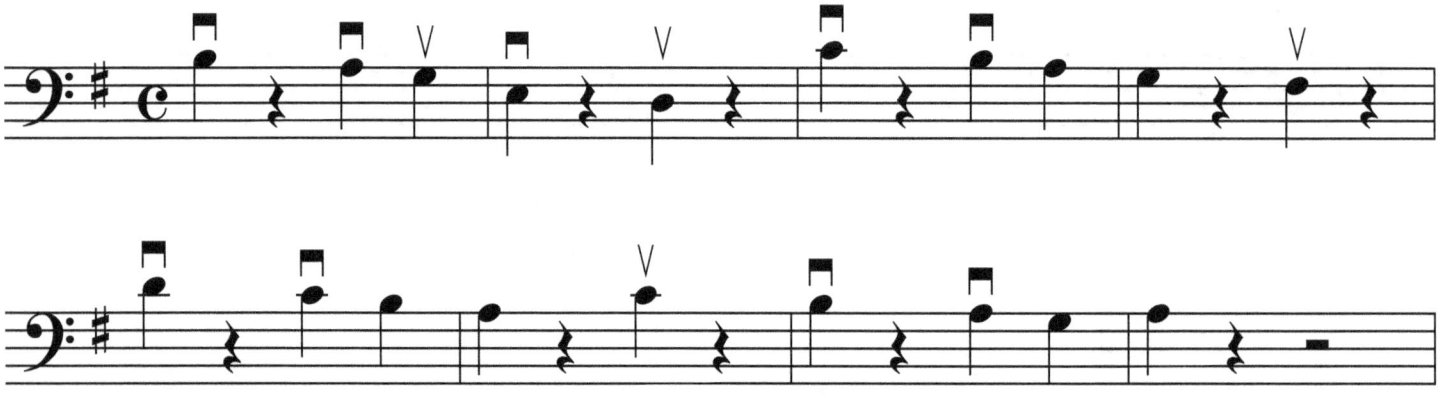

Cello Etude System, Book 0: Solo Book

112. Study in 7/4
C. Harvey

Flatten first finger across two strings.

Accelerated students may skip to No. 114.

©2021 C. Harvey Publications All Rights Reserved

113. G Major Staccato Study

E. Depas, arr. Harvey

114. G Major Double Stop Etude

J. de Swert, arr. Harvey

115. Second and Third Finger

C. Harvey

116. Learning a Slow Up-Bow

C. Harvey

117. Etude in Folk Style

F. Bornschein, arr. Harvey

Cello Etude System, Book 0: Solo Book

118. Slurs and Rhythm

H. Goodban, arr. Harvey

119. Bow Rhythm Etude

A. Cuccoli, arr. Harvey

120. Rhythmic Etude

B. Stiastny, arr. Harvey

Index of Composers

Etude(s)

Bornschein, Franz	16,40,42,44,49,51,67,69,73,117
Chevillard, Alexandre	99
Cousin, Émile	83,106-107
Cuccoli, Arturo	98,103-104,119
Davidov, Karl	7,33,39,52,58,64
Depas, Ernest	113
de Swert, Jules	92,114
Duport, J. V.	102
Fuchs, Carl	4,72,76,109
Goodban, Henry	118
Gruet, Albert	100
Harvey, Cassia	2,12,14,15,17,19-24,26-30,35,37-38,41,43,48, 50,54-57,60,62-63,65-66,68,70-71,80,82, 84-86,88-90,108,112,115-116
Kummer, Friedrich	9,91
Liégeois, Cornélis	13,101
Mazas, Jacques	81
Mollier, P.	95-96,111
Nölck, August	31,45,53,59,78,94
Paschalski, Konstanty	105
Romberg, Bernhard	32,34,77,79
Schiffer, Adolf	18,36,46-47
Schröder, Carl	5,87
Stiastny, Bernard	120
Uberti, V.	110
van Rooijen, N. F.	93,97
Verrimst, Victor	8,25
Werner, Josef	3
Whitehouse, William	74,75
Wichtl, Georg	1,6,10,11,61

Index of Main Skills in Each Etude

	Etude(s)
Agility/Speed	38,43,55,62,66-67,82,98,102
Bow Speed	5-8,10-11,13,20,24-25,36,39,44,54,61,73-75, 91-93,103,116-120
Bowing; Pickup Notes	70-71,96-87
Bowing; Retaking bows	85,89,111
Bowing; Slurs	15-19,21,29,35-36,40,42,48-49,69,73,80-81, 90,101,107,109-110,117-118
Bowing; Staccato	78-81,83,104,113
Bowing; String Crossing	1-2,5,9,12-13,15-21,25,48,68,80-81,83,96, 106
Bowing; Ties	39-40,100,103
Bowing; Up-Bows	44,95-97,110
Double Stops	4,19,21,67,77,82,88-89,94,105,114
Dynamics	14,83,91-92,101
Learning Notes	1-2,26,31,37,40,47,53,57,59,63,86,108
Melodic Etudes	41,46-47,62,99
Reading Notes	27-28,30,32-34,38,52,54-55,58,64,90,109, 115,117,119
Rhythm Skills, General	7-8,10-11,20,24-25,28,36,39,60,72,93,112,120
Rhythm, 6/8	22-23,56,65,84,102
Rhythm, 3/4	9,42,50-51,67,73-75,87,91-92
Tone	3,4,45,54,59,72,76,94

available from **www.charveypublications.com**: CHP305

Beginning Fiddle Duets for Two Cellos

Cripple Creek

Trad., arr. Myanna Harvey

©2016 C. Harvey Publications All Rights Reserved.